Gifted & Talented®

Science
Questions & Answers

THE OCEAN

For Ages 6–8

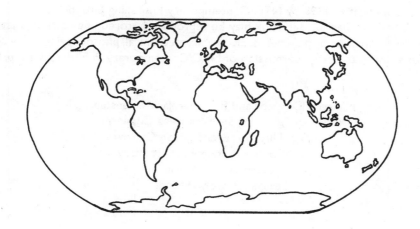

By Barbara Saffer, Ph.D.

Illustrated by Kerry Manwaring

LOWELL HOUSE JUVENILE

LOS ANGELES

NTC/Contemporary Publishing Group

Published by Lowell House
A division of NTC/Contemporary Publishing Group, Inc.
4255 West Touhy Avenue, Lincolnwood (Chicago), Illinois 60712 U.S.A.

Managing Director and Publisher: Jack Artenstein
Director of Publishing Services: Rena Copperman
Editorial Director: Brenda Pope-Ostrow
Director of Art Production: Bret Perry
Editor: Linda Gorman
Designer: Carolyn Wendt

Lowell House books can be purchased at special discounts
when ordered in bulk for premiums and special sales.
Please contact Customer Service at:
NTC/Contemporary Publishing Group
4255 W. Touhy Avenue
Lincolnwood, IL 60712
1-800-323-4900

Printed and bound in the United States of America

Library of Congress Catalog Card Number: 99-94549

ISBN: 0-7373-0210-0

ML 10 9 8 7 6 5 4 3 2 1

Note to Parents

Teach a child facts and you give her knowledge. Teach her to think and you give her wisdom. This is the principle behind the entire series of *Gifted & Talented*® materials. And this is the reason that thinking skills are being stressed in classrooms throughout the country.

The questions and answers in the **Gifted & Talented® Question & Answer** books have been designed specifically to promote the development of critical and creative thinking skills. Each page features one "topic question" that is answered above a corresponding picture. This topic provides the springboard to the following questions on the page.

Each of these six related questions focuses on a different higher-level thinking skill. The skills include knowledge and recall, comprehension, deduction, inference, sequencing, prediction, classification, analyzing, problem solving, and creative expansion.

The topic question, answer, and artwork contain the answers or clues to the answers for some of the other questions. Certain questions, however, can only be answered by relating the topic to other facts that your child may already know. At the back of the book are suggested answers to help you guide your child.

Effective questioning has been used to develop a child's intellectual gifts since the time of Socrates. Certainly, it is the most common teaching technique in classrooms today. But asking questions isn't as easy as it looks! On the following page you will find a few tips to keep in mind that will help you and your child use this book more effectively.

★ First of all, let your child flip through the book and select the questions and pictures that interest him or her. If the child wants to do only one page, that's fine. If he or she wants to answer only some of the questions on a page, save the others for another time.

★ Give your child time to think! Wait at least 10 seconds before you offer any help. You'd be surprised how little time many parents and teachers give a child to think before jumping right in and answering a question themselves.

★ Help your child by restating or rephrasing the question if necessary. But again, make sure you pause and give the child time to answer first. Also, don't ask the same question over and over! Go on to another question, or use hints to prompt your child when needed.

★ Encourage your child to give more details or expand upon answers by asking questions such as "What made you say that?" or "Why do you think so?"

★ This book will not only teach your child about many things, but it will teach *you* a lot about your child. Make the most of your time together—and have fun!

The answers at the back of the book are to be used as a guide. Sometimes your child may come up with an answer that is different but still a good answer. Remember, the principle behind all *Gifted & Talented*® materials is to **teach your child to think**—not just to give answers.

Why is Earth sometimes called *the blue planet*?

Earth is sometimes called *the blue planet* because in pictures taken from space, the Earth looks blue. The blue color is water, which covers almost three-quarters of the planet's surface. Most of Earth's water is contained in the oceans. Oceans make life possible on our planet. They provide rainwater for plants and food for animals. In addition, tiny ocean plants called *algae* (AL-jee) produce most of the world's oxygen. Earth is the only planet in our solar system known to have large amounts of water.

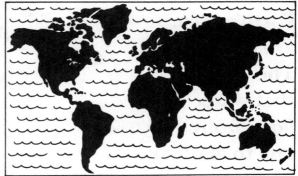

■ Land ⊞ Water

1. Look at a globe or a map of the Earth. What color is used to show water?
2. Do you think a ship could travel around the world without touching land?
3. Some people say our planet should be called "Ocean" instead of "Earth." Why do you think they say this?
4. Why do parts of the ocean sometimes look green?
5. Why is it important for people that algae produce oxygen?
6. Almost all of the water on Earth is in the oceans. Where do you think the rest is?

How many oceans are there?

Geographers (jee-OGG-ruh-fers), people who study the Earth's natural features, don't all agree on how many oceans there are. Some geographers say there are five oceans. From largest to smallest, they are the Pacific, Atlantic, Indian, Antarctic, and Arctic. Other geographers say there are three oceans: the Pacific, Atlantic, and Indian. They consider the Antarctic and Arctic oceans to be part of the other oceans. All of the Earth's oceans are connected. This means that water flows from one to another.

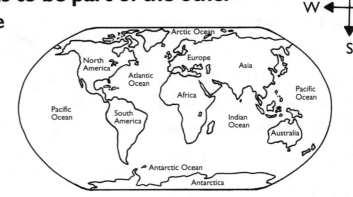

1. Which of Earth's oceans covers the biggest area?
2. Which two oceans, or parts of oceans, have the coldest water? Why?
3. Look at the map on this page. Which ocean is west of Europe? Which ocean is east of Africa?
4. Some people say the Earth really has only one big ocean. Why do you think they say this?
5. What other natural features do geographers study?
6. If you were asked to re-name the oceans, what would you call them?

How did the oceans form?

About 4 and a half billion years ago, hot gas and dust particles circling the Sun smashed together to form the planets. A sizzling, waterless Earth was created. As the Earth cooled, a gas called *water vapor* was released. The water vapor came together, or *condensed,* into droplets. These droplets then formed clouds. Rain from the clouds slowly filled low areas in the land. These areas became the first oceans.

1. Which is bigger, a million or a billion?
2. What does **sizzling** mean?
3. Look at a map or a globe. Which ocean did Columbus cross when he traveled from Spain to America?
4. Which state in the United States is located in the Pacific Ocean?
5. What happens when an area on land gets too much rain?
6. Scientists believe that life began in the oceans. What do you think the first living things on Earth looked like?

7

What is the water cycle?

The Earth's water doesn't stay in one place. The Sun constantly heats the water in oceans, lakes, rivers, and streams. Some of the water *evaporates,* becoming a gas called *water vapor.* Water vapor rises into the atmosphere. There it comes together, or *condenses,* into water droplets. These droplets form clouds. Water from clouds falls back to Earth as *precipitation* in the form of rain or snow. Some water falls directly into oceans, lakes, and streams. Other water seeps into the ground to form groundwater. Most of the groundwater eventually trickles back to rivers, which return it to the oceans. This whole process, which occurs over and over again, is called the *water cycle.*

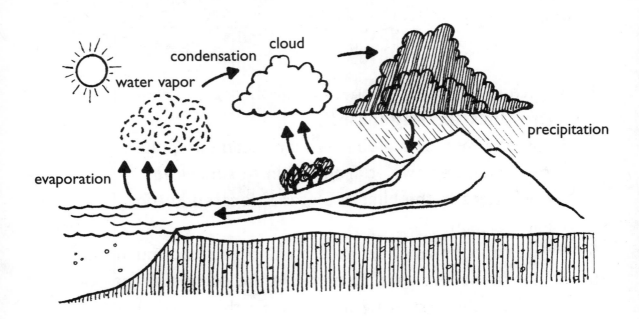

1. What is a cycle?
2. What are clouds made of?
3. Groundwater is an important source of drinking water. How do you think people get groundwater out of the ground?
4. What do we call clouds that are close to the ground?
5. What is the difference between evaporation and condensation?
6. Sometimes the water cycle adds pollution to the land. How do you think this happens?

One Step Further

With an adult's help, pour 2 cups of very hot water into a bowl. *Do not touch the water with your hand.* Hold a small mirror over the bowl while you slowly count to 30. What happens to the mirror?

Is the ocean floor flat?

Parts of the ocean floor are flat. These areas are called *abyssal* (ah-BIH-sul) plains. However, the ocean floor also has tall mountains and deep canyons. These features form because the Earth's crust is made of separate pieces called *plates*. The plates can break and move around. When the ocean floor cracks, hot melted rock from inside the Earth oozes up to form mountains or volcanoes. When one plate slides beneath another plate, a canyon, or *trench*, is created.

1. What kinds of features are found on the ocean floor?
2. How are abyssal plains like grassy plains on land?
3. Can you name some mountains that are found on land?
4. Many small islands in the ocean are really just the tops of underwater mountains or volcanoes. Look at a map or a globe. What are some islands in the ocean?
5. What do you think happens when two plates of the Earth's crust smash together?
6. The Moon has no oceans. Do you think the Moon is completely smooth?

What are continental margins?

Continental margins are the areas around the edges of the continents, where the seafloor slopes from the coast to the deep sea. A continental margin has three parts: the shelf, the slope, and the rise. The continental shelf is the gently slanted area next to the land. The shelf ends at the continental slope, which plunges steeply downward. The continental rise is a thick layer of sand and mud that stretches from the continental slope to the deep-sea floor.

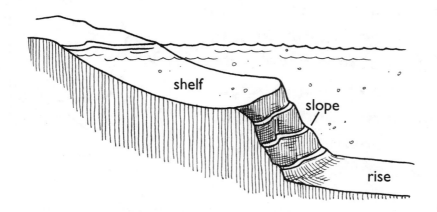

1. Which part of the continental margin is closest to a beach?
2. What does **plunge** mean?
3. How is a continental slope like a cliff on land?
4. What do people use shelves for?
5. Look at a map or a globe. Can you name a city on each continent that is near a continental margin?
6. Some parts of the world have ice shelves. What do you think these are? Where do you think they're found?

How deep is the ocean?

The depth of the ocean changes from one area to another. The flat parts of the seafloor are called the *abyssal* (ah-BIH-sul) plains. In the Atlantic Ocean, the abyssal plains are about 12,000 feet deep. In the Pacific Ocean, they are about 13,800 feet deep. Ocean trenches—long, narrow underwater canyons—are much deeper. The deepest trench on Earth, the Mariana Trench in the Pacific Ocean, is 36,198 feet (almost 7 miles) deep! Some animals, such as sea cucumbers and jellyfish, live at the bottom of the Mariana Trench.

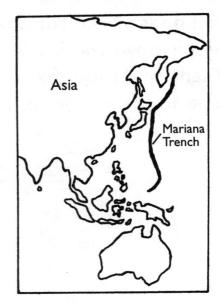

Asia

Mariana Trench

1. Which ocean is deeper, the Atlantic or the Pacific?
2. Look at a map or a globe. What countries are closest to the Mariana Trench?
3. Do you think the abyssal plains are well lit or dark? warm or cold?
4. Do you think plants can live on the abyssal plains? Why or why not?
5. Can you name a deep canyon on land?
6. How do you think scientists study the bottom of the ocean?

What is oceanography?

Oceanography (OH-shih-NAH-grah-fee) is the scientific study of the oceans. The first expedition to explore the ocean depths set sail on the HMS *Challenger* in 1872. The voyagers mapped the seafloor and collected many kinds of ocean life. Today, researchers use *submersibles,* or small submarines, to study the oceans. Other instruments oceanographers use include sonar (sound waves), to map the ocean floor; camera sleds, to take pictures of the ocean floor; and space satellites, to study waves and currents and to measure the temperature of the water.

1. What is an oceanographer?
2. What do scientists study in the oceans?
3. Why is it easier to study the oceans today than it was in 1872?
4. How do you think a navy submarine is different from a submersible?
5. Why do you think it's important to study the oceans?
6. Would you like to visit the ocean depths in a submersible? Why or why not?

Why is ocean water salty?

Ocean water is salty because it contains large amounts of *sodium chloride,* or common salt. The salt comes from the land. Ocean water constantly evaporates into the air, forms clouds, and falls as rain. As rainwater runs over rocks and through soil, it picks up salt. In time, the water and salt flow back to the oceans. Over billions of years, the oceans have become very salty. People have used salt from the oceans for thousands of years. To obtain the salt, people flood shallow ponds, called *salt pans,* with seawater. When the seawater evaporates, salt is left behind.

1. How does salt get into the oceans?
2. What do people use salt for?
3. Can you name some salty foods?
4. Why is water in rivers and lakes called *fresh water*?
5. Salt pans are usually found in places with hot weather. Look at a map or a globe. Which countries do you think might have salt pans?
6. A person who is stranded on a lifeboat in the ocean can die of thirst. Why do you think this is?

One Step Further

Pour warm water into a shallow aluminum pie pan until it's about three-quarters full. Add 2 or 3 tablespoons of salt. Stir the water until the salt dissolves, or "disappears" in the water. Put the pan in a warm, dry place and leave it there. After several days, check the pan. What do you find? Can you explain your results?

What is the difference between an ocean and a sea?

The words *ocean* and *sea* are both used to describe large bodies of salt water. However, they are not exactly the same. Oceans are larger than seas. In fact, some seas are just parts of oceans. For example, the Arabian Sea is part of the Indian Ocean. Other seas are surrounded by continents. These seas are usually connected to oceans by passages called *channels*.

For instance, the Mediterranean Sea, between Europe and Africa, is connected to the Atlantic Ocean by the Strait of Gibraltar. There are at least 50 named seas.

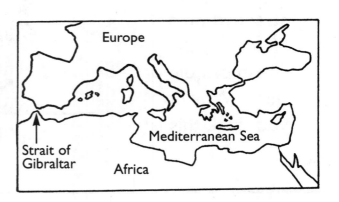

1. What is the major difference between an ocean and a sea?
2. Does the world have more oceans or more seas?
3. Find the Caribbean Sea on a map or a globe. Which ocean is it part of?
4. Find the Red Sea on a map or a globe. Which continents surround it?
5. What are some animals whose names have the word **sea** in them?
6. What is the difference between a lake and a sea?

How did the Dead Sea, Black Sea, and Red Sea get their names?

The Dead Sea, in southwestern Asia, is in a hot climate. Water in the Dead Sea evaporates constantly, leaving salt behind. Almost no living things can survive in such salty water, so it's called the Dead Sea. The Black Sea, between Europe and Asia, has little oxygen in its bottom waters. The bacteria that live in those waters produce a chemical called *hydrogen sulfide*. This makes the sea look black. The Red Sea, between Africa and Asia, gets its name from the red *algae* (AL-jee) that grow on its surface.

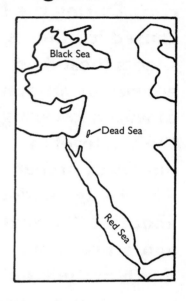

1. Why are there almost no plants or animals in the Dead Sea?
2. Look at a map or a globe. What are some countries around the Black Sea?
3. Lakes and swamps sometimes smell like hydrogen sulfide, or rotten eggs. Do these waters have a lot of oxygen or a little?
4. What is seasickness?
5. Why do you think it's very easy to float in the Dead Sea?
6. The White Sea is south of the Arctic Ocean, near Russia. How do you think it got its name?

How does sea level change?

Sea level is the level of the ocean where the ocean meets land. Sea level changes when the amount of water in the ocean changes. This usually occurs when seawater freezes or melts as the temperature falls or rises. During the last ice age, a drop in temperature caused ice sheets to form all over the world. The ice sheets locked up enormous amounts of water, lowering the sea level by hundreds of feet. The ice age ended about 10,000 years ago. Since then, the Earth has gotten warmer, and most of the ice sheets have melted. As a result, the sea level has risen.

1. Has sea level always been the same as it is now?

2. The Earth still has some ice sheets. Where do you think they are?

3. Why do you think the fossils of prehistoric animals are sometimes found underwater?

4. What do you think causes ice ages?

5. Many scientists believe that the Earth's temperature is rising because of pollution in the atmosphere. What do you think might happen if the Earth gets much warmer?

6. Woolly mammoths were elephant-like animals that lived during the last ice age. What do you think they looked like? Draw your picture on a separate piece of paper.

One Step Further

Scientists believe that air pollution in the atmosphere is causing the Earth's temperature to rise by holding in heat. This is called the *greenhouse effect.* To demonstrate the greenhouse effect, try this simple experiment. Get two identical glass jars. Put 1 cup of cold water and five ice cubes in each jar. Place one jar in a large zipper-lock plastic bag and seal the bag; this jar is the "greenhouse jar." The plastic bag *represents,* or stands for, air pollution in the Earth's atmosphere. Set both jars in the sun or under a hot lamp for two hours. Then measure the water temperature in each jar with a thermometer. What are your results? Can you explain them?

What is an estuary?

An estuary forms where a river meets a sea. In an estuary, fresh water from the river mixes with salt water from the sea, creating an unusual environment. Many estuaries are muddy areas with sea grasses, seaweeds, and mangrove trees. Unlike most trees, mangroves can grow in muddy, salty water. Estuaries are a good source of food for animals, and many fish hatch and grow there. Various kinds of worms, crabs, clams, mussels, and snails also live in estuaries, and seabirds often stop by to find food.

1. How is an estuary different from the open sea?
2. Can you name some kinds of trees, other than mangroves?
3. What are the names of some well-known rivers?
4. Lighthouses are sometimes built near estuaries. Why are lighthouses important to sailors?
5. If you had to prepare a meal made entirely of food that grows in estuaries, what would you serve?
6. Many pollutants, such as garbage, chemicals, and oil, get into estuaries. How do you think this affects estuaries? How would you clean them up?

What are tides?

On most coasts, sea level changes four times a day. These changes are called *tides*. Tides are caused by the *gravitational* (gra-vih-TAY-shun-ul) *attraction,* or pulling force, of the Moon. As the Earth *rotates,* or turns, the waters nearest the Moon are pulled into a bulge called a *high tide.* Because of the Earth's rotation, a high tide also forms on the opposite side of the Earth. Areas between the bulges have low water levels, called *low tides.* Tides change about every six hours, in a cycle of high tide, low tide, high tide, low tide.

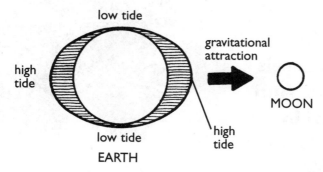

1. How many low tides does a coast have in one day?
2. What is a bulge?
3. Imagine you're sitting on a beach and the ocean is getting closer to you. What's happening?
4. How do high tides help large ships enter or leave ports?
5. When is the best time to look for seashells on a beach? Why?
6. The Sun affects the tides too, but much less than the Moon does. Why do you think this is?

What is a tide pool?

Like other coastal areas, rocky shores are covered by high tides twice a day. When the tide goes out, water trapped between rocks forms tide pools. Every tide pool contains a community of plants and animals. The plants are usually small *algae* (AL-jee) and seaweeds. Many different animals live in tide pools.

Sea stars, sea *anemones* (ah-NEH-mah-nees), and crabs live on the bottom. Snails crawl on stones and plants. Barnacles, oysters, and mussels attach to rocks. And small fish swim in the water.

1. Could you visit a tide pool during high tide?
2. Where do the animals in a tide pool live?
3. How do you think seaweeds are useful to animals in tide pools?
4. Why do tide pools form on rocky shores rather than sandy shores?
5. Do you think all tide pools have the same kinds of plants and animals?
6. How do you think plants and animals get into tide pools?

How are waves made?

Most waves are created by the wind. When wind blows over the ocean, it makes ripples in the water. These ripples, or waves, travel across the ocean until they break on a shore. The size of a wave depends on how fast, how long, and how far the wind blows. A wave doesn't actually push water along. As the energy of a wave moves across the ocean, water bobs up and down, but it doesn't move forward. It is like what happens when you shake a rope. A wave travels through the rope, but the rope itself doesn't move forward.

1. What determines the size of a wave?
2. How high do you think waves created by the wind can get?
3. Why are waves sometimes dangerous to sailors?
4. Do you think a wave could move a bottle across the ocean?
5. Do you think waves affect the bottom of the ocean?
6. Strong waves can change the shape of a coastline. How do you think this happens?

What are currents?

Currents are enormous bands of water that move through the oceans. *Surface currents* flow near the top of the ocean. They are controlled by winds, the locations of the continents, and the Earth's spin. Surface currents travel in clockwise circles north of the equator and in counterclockwise circles south of the equator. *Deep-water currents* are caused by differences in water *density*, or weight. Deep currents start at the north and south poles, which have very cold, salty, dense water. Polar water sinks to the ocean floor and flows toward the equator. Warmer, lighter water then moves in to replace it. Eventually, currents exchange top and bottom water in all the oceans.

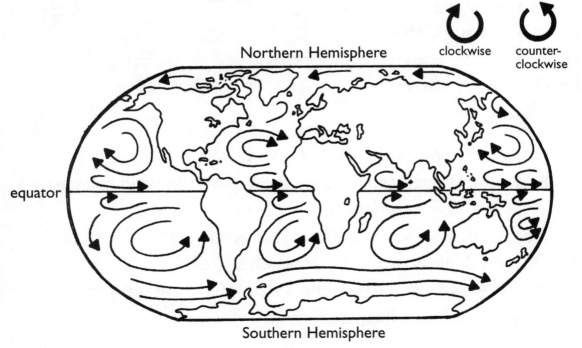

Northern Hemisphere

clockwise   counter-clockwise

equator

Southern Hemisphere

1. What is the difference between surface currents and deep-water currents?
2. Do all the oceans have currents?
3. How can currents be dangerous to swimmers?
4. Why do you think currents are sometimes called "rivers of the sea"?
5. When a river meets an ocean, the river water flows over the ocean water. Why do you think this is?
6. Several years ago, thousands of sneakers were swept off a ship in the Pacific Ocean. How do you think the shoes helped scientists study ocean currents?

One Step Further

With an adult's help, try this activity to see how dense water flows beneath less dense water.

1. Prepare dense water: Pour 4 cups of tap water into a large glass bowl. Stir in ⅓ cup of salt. Add 20 ice cubes to the bowl and stir the water until the ice melts. The water should be icy cold.
2. Prepare the light water: Pour ½ cup of very hot tap water into a glass and stir in 2 drops of food coloring.
3. Combine the two kinds of water: *Very gently* pour the hot water over the side of the glass bowl containing the cold water.

What happens? How is this like the ocean currents?

? How does the ocean affect the weather?

Ocean currents influence *climate,* or long-term weather. For example, the **Gulf Stream** is a warm current that flows around the northern Atlantic Ocean. It brings mild weather to eastern parts of the United States and western Europe. The cold **California current**, on the other hand, produces fog over western parts of the United States. Oceans also cause savage storms.

Winds above warm seas, for instance, can become twisting masses of wet air. The swirling winds may form violent hurricanes or seagoing tornadoes called *waterspouts.*

1. What is the climate like where you live?
2. Look at a map or a globe. Which states *border,* or are next to, California?
3. What are some words used to describe weather?
4. What are some kinds of storms other than hurricanes?
5. Why are some currents warm and others cold?
6. The study of weather is called *meteorology* (MEE-tee-or-OHL-ah-jee). Can you think of some other words that end with *-ology*?

What is El Niño?

El Niño (NEEN-yoh) is a change in wind patterns. Normally, winds along the equator push warm water to the western Pacific Ocean. During an El Niño, however, the winds change direction and push warm water to the eastern Pacific Ocean. The warm water reduces the flow of nutrients into the eastern Pacific. This reduces the food supply for sea animals. The warm water is also picked up by the atmosphere. This causes hurricanes near the eastern Pacific and dry spells near the western Pacific. El Niños last for a year or two.

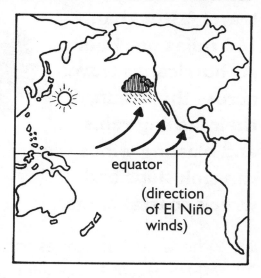

equator

(direction of El Niño winds)

1. What causes an El Niño?
2. Has an El Niño ever affected the area where you live?
3. Look at a map or a globe. What are some countries along the eastern Pacific Ocean? the western Pacific Ocean?
4. How do you think El Niño hurts the fishing industry in the eastern Pacific?
5. El Niño dry spells can cause serious damage. What are some effects of dry spells?
6. Why do people all over the world become concerned when scientists predict an El Niño?

What is a hurricane?

A hurricane is a violent, circular storm. Hurricanes start near the equator, when warm, moist air rises from the ocean's surface. The climbing air swirls around because of the Earth's spin. As more and more wet air spirals upward, huge rain clouds form and wind speed increases. The winds of a strong hurricane can travel faster than 150 miles per hour. As hurricanes travel across the ocean, their lashing rains and blasting winds can sink ships and wreck coastal areas.

1. Where do hurricanes form?
2. Which travel faster, cars on a highway or the strong winds of a hurricane?
3. What are storm warnings?
4. Why are storm warnings sent out?
5. If you heard that a hurricane was coming toward your home, how would you prepare for it?
6. Hurricanes are given the names of girls and boys, in alternating order (girl, boy, girl, boy, etc.). Can you make up a list of hurricane names from A to Z? Write your names on a separate piece of paper.

What is a waterspout?

A waterspout is a whirling column of air that hangs down from clouds over water. Waterspouts usually develop over warm seas. When the twisting air of a waterspout touches the ocean, it sucks up moisture and becomes a watery tornado. A waterspout travels across the sea with its cloud, which may be thousands of feet above the water's surface. If the column of water is released suddenly, it can wreck ships and destroy areas along the coastline.

1. Do many waterspouts form over the Arctic Ocean?
2. What does **whirling** mean?
3. What do you think a whirlpool is?
4. How are a waterspout and a tornado alike? How are they different?
5. What did a tornado do in *The Wizard of Oz*?
6. Do you think waterspouts ever carry anything besides water?

What is a tidal wave?

A tidal wave, or *tsunami* (tsoo-NAH-mee), is an enormous ocean wave created by an undersea earthquake, landslide, or volcanic eruption. A tsunami has nothing to do with the tides. Tsunamis can travel thousands of miles and may reach speeds of 600 miles per hour. In the open sea, a tsunami may be less than 2 feet high. But when a tsunami reaches a distant shore, it can form a gigantic wave over 100 feet high. Tsunamis often destroy coastal areas.

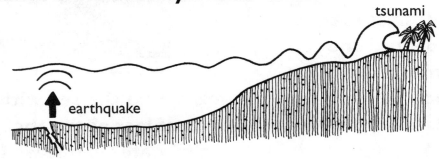

tsunami

earthquake

1. What causes a tsunami?
2. *Tsunami* means "harbor wave" in Japanese. Why is this a better name than *tidal wave*?
3. If a tsunami is moving at 600 miles per hour, how far will it travel in 30 minutes?
4. In 1998, a tsunami destroyed many villages in Papua New Guinea. Can you find Papua New Guinea on a map or a globe? What ocean is it in?
5. Do you think a tsunami can be predicted?
6. How can people figure out how high a tsunami was?

What is a riptide?

A riptide has nothing to do with the tides and is properly called a *rip current*. A rip current is a narrow, fast-moving flow of water rushing from the shore out to sea. Rip currents form when water swept onto the shore is trapped by a sandbar, a reef, or other underwater obstacle. The water funnels out through an opening in the obstacle, creating a powerful, seagoing current. Rip currents can be dangerous to swimmers because they can pull them away from shore.

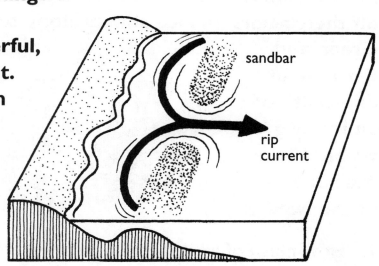

1. Why is *riptide* not a good name for a rip current?
2. Which direction does a rip current travel?
3. What does **funnel** mean?
4. How could you spot a rip current from shore?
5. What should you do if you get caught in a rip current?
6. What are some things people do at the beach?

How do icebergs form?

Icebergs are produced when enormous chunks of ice break off from ice sheets and "rivers" of ice called *glaciers*. The breaking process is called *calving*. Icebergs are found in the Antarctic, Arctic, and North Atlantic oceans. Antarctic icebergs calve off the gigantic ice cap that covers the Antarctic continent. Most of the Arctic and North Atlantic icebergs calve off the glaciers and ice sheets along the coast of Greenland.

Only about one-tenth of an iceberg is visible above the surface of the water.

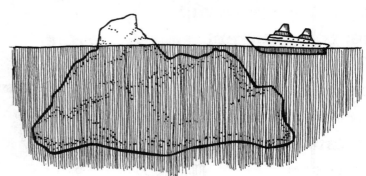

1. How much of an iceberg is underwater?
2. Why are icebergs dangerous to ships?
3. What famous ship sank after hitting an iceberg?
4. What kind of ship do you think an icebreaker is? What do you think it's used for?
5. Can you name some animals that live in the Arctic? in the Antarctic?
6. What do you think might happen if all the ice sheets and icebergs in the world melted?

What are coral reefs?

Coral reefs are large stony structures found in warm, shallow seas. Coral reefs are built by tiny animals called *polyps* (POL-ips). Coral polyps live in huge colonies. Each animal in the colony builds a bonelike limestone cup around itself. When the polyp dies, the limestone cup remains behind. A new polyp then grows on top of it. After many years, millions of limestone cups accumulate to form a coral reef. Coral reefs swarm with many kinds of colorful sea life, including fish, anemones, eels, and sea stars.

1. Do you think a limestone cup is hard or soft?
2. Are there any coral reefs in the Arctic Ocean? Why?
3. What do you think brain coral is?
4. How does a coral reef help small fish?
5. What is the difference between **coral** and **corral**?
6. Small plants called *algae* live inside coral polyps and help them grow. How do you think the algae help the polyps? How do you think the polyps help the algae?

What is the Great Barrier Reef?

The Great Barrier Reef is the largest coral reef in the world. About 1,250 miles long, the reef is actually made up of many smaller reefs that run along the northeast coast of Australia. Hundreds of different kinds of coral and fish live on the reef, along with clams, sea turtles, and birds. The Great Barrier Reef is one of Australia's most popular tourist attractions. In 1976, most of the reef was declared a national marine park to protect it from the damage being done by visitors and pollution.

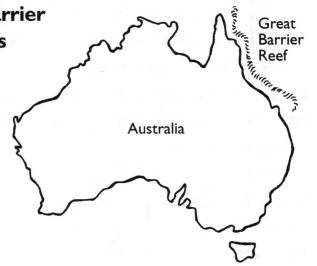

1. Find the Great Barrier Reef on a map or a globe. What country, after Australia, is closest to it?
2. What is a marine park?
3. Coral reefs grow only about 2 inches per year. How long would it take a reef to grow 1 foot?
4. What are some famous tourist attractions in the United States?
5. How do visitors and pollution hurt coral reefs?
6. Why do you think it is called the Great *Barrier* Reef?

What are plankton?

Plankton are tiny plants and animals that swim or drift in the upper ocean. Most plankton are too small to be seen without a microscope. Populations of plant plankton, called *phytoplankton* (fi-toh-**PLANK**-ton), include various kinds of *algae* (**AL**-jee).

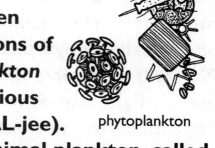

phytoplankton

Populations of animal plankton, called *zooplankton* (zoh-uh-**PLANK**-ton), include tiny shrimp, young crabs, and baby fish. The ocean contains an enormous number of plankton, which are an important source of food for larger creatures.

zooplankton

1. What is the difference between phytoplankton and zooplankton?
2. What does a microscope do?
3. Can you name some large sea plants?
4. Why do you think most sea plants don't need roots?
5. Do you think plankton could be used to feed all the hungry people in the world?
6. If all the plankton disappeared from the ocean, what do you think would happen?

What is an ocean food chain?

All living things are part of a food chain. Each member of a food chain is a meal for the next member. In the ocean, the food chain starts with tiny plants called *phytoplankton* (fi-toh-PLANK-ton). Phytoplankton live in the upper ocean, where they use sunlight and other elements to make food. Phytoplankton are eaten by small animals called *zooplankton* (zoh-uh-PLANK-ton). Zooplankton, such as jellyfish and *copepods* (KOH-puh-pods), are eaten in turn by larger animals, such as fish and squid. Fish and squid are devoured by even bigger creatures, such as sharks and killer whales. When ocean creatures die, they are eaten by *scavengers,* including catfish and crabs. Any remaining soft parts of dead animals are broken down by bacteria called *decomposers.*

1. Are human beings part of a food chain?
2. Why don't phytoplankton live in the deep sea?

3. An *herbivore* (ER-buh-vor) is a plant-eater. What do you think a *carnivore* (CAR-nuh-vor) is?
4. What do you think the *top predator* of a food chain is?
5. Why are decomposers important to a food chain?
6. Imagine that an oil spill killed all the baby fish in an area. How do you think this would affect the food chain?

One Step Further

Follow these directions to make your own food chains.

- Get sheets of construction paper in the following colors: green, yellow, red, brown, and black. Cut strips, 1 inch wide, from the short sides of the papers. Draw or paste pictures of plants on the green strips, plant-eaters on the yellow strips, small meat-eaters on the red strips, large meat-eaters on the brown strips, and scavengers on the black strips. Use pictures of sea creatures, land creatures, or both.

- Make a paper "food chain" by linking the appropriate strips into a chain. An example of a land-based food chain is: leaf (on green paper)—caterpillar (on yellow paper)—bird (on red paper)—snake (on brown paper)—owl (on brown paper)—vulture (on black paper).

What kinds of animals live along the shore?

Different types of animals live on different types of shores. Creatures that live on *sandy shores* **burrow into the soft sand to protect themselves from predators. Inhabitants of sandy shores include crabs, clams, and sand dollars.** *Rocky shores* **occur where currents sweep away sand and mud. Because of the strong water movement, animals here must cling to rocks or hide in crevices. They include sea urchins, lobsters, sea stars, rock crabs, jellyfish, barnacles, and mussels.**

1. What kind of shore do you find at a swimming beach?
2. What is a predator?
3. Could you walk along a sandy shore without seeing any animals?
4. Sea otters sometimes eat shellfish. How do they crack them open?
5. A crab's shell doesn't grow with its body. How do you think a small crab becomes a large crab?
6. How do the tides make life difficult for animals along the shore?

What are fish?

Fish are *vertebrates* (VUR-tuh-brets), or animals with backbones. They live in water. Fish have fins for swimming, gills for breathing, and scale-covered skin. They usually lay eggs to produce young. Most fish have a gas-filled swim bladder to help them float. The fish *inflate,* or fill, the swim bladder to go up and *deflate,* or empty, the swim bladder to go down. Sharks don't have swim bladders and must swim constantly to keep from sinking. There are about 22,000 kinds of fish of various sizes, shapes, and colors.

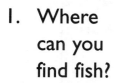

1. Where can you find fish?
2. What other animals lay eggs to produce young?
3. What are some fish that people eat?
4. Besides fish, what other animals are vertebrates?
5. Some people use the name *sea star* instead of *starfish.* Why do you think they use this name?
6. Fish sometimes make sounds by vibrating their swim bladders. Why do you think they do this?

How do fish swim?

Most fish swim by sweeping their tails from side to side. This motion pushes the fish forward. Most fish use their fins to control their direction and to stop. Many fish are long and narrow, or *streamlined,* to reduce water resistance, or drag.

caudal fin (tail) dorsal fin pectoral fin

anal fin pelvic fin

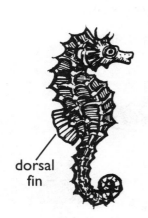

dorsal fin

Not all fish use their tails for swimming. Seahorses use their *dorsal,* or back, fins to swim. Long, thin eels wriggle through the water like snakes. And a few fish, such as walking catfish, "walk" along the seabed with their fins.

1. What is another name for a fish's tail?
2. Which fins do you think a fish uses to turn and stop?
3. What do you think flying fish are?
4. What do we mean when we say that someone "swims like a fish"?
5. When swimming at top speed, a fish may hold its fins against its body. Why do you think it does this?
6. Besides fish, can you name some other things that are streamlined?

How do fish breathe?

Like other animals, fish breathe to get oxygen. Oxygen is used for *respiration,* a process that produces energy for the body. To obtain oxygen, a fish takes water into its mouth and pumps it back over its *gills.* Gills are thin tissues filled with blood vessels. Blood in the gills picks up oxygen from the water. Blood also passes *carbon dioxide,* a waste product of respiration, back into the water. The water then flows out of the fish through its gill openings.

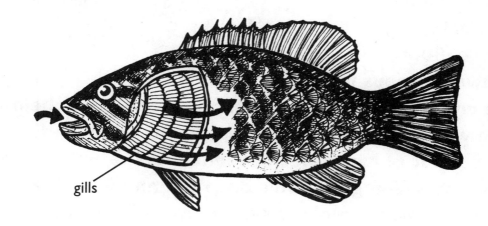

gills

1. How do people get oxygen?
2. What organ pumps blood through a fish's body?
3. How are the lungs of land animals similar to gills?
4. How are lungs and gills different?
5. What do you think lungfish are?
6. Young frogs, called *tadpoles,* have gills and adult frogs have lungs. Why do you think this is?

What are black smokers?

Black smokers are dark chimneys that form on the bottom of the ocean around *hydrothermal vents.* Hydrothermal vents are "escape passages" that form around cracks in the seafloor. Seawater seeps into the cracks and flows through hot melted rock below. The water gets scalding hot, picks up sulfur, and shoots out of hydrothermal vents. As the water cools, sulfur-containing minerals drop out and form black smokers. Black smokers can be over 65 feet tall.

1. What are black smokers made of?
2. What does **scalding** mean?
3. Are any jets of hot water found on land?
4. Why does a fireplace need to have a chimney?
5. Why do you think hydrothermal vents are called *smokers?*
6. What do you think white smokers are?

Are there plants in the deep sea?

No, there are no plants at the bottom of the sea. Plants need sunlight, but sunlight cannot reach the ocean depths. This makes the ocean floor a very cold, dark place. However, some animals are able to survive in the deep sea. Deep-sea bacteria use sulfur from black smokers to make food.

Creatures such as giant clams and tube worms have bacteria in their bodies. They use food the bacteria make. Other animals, such as shrimp, eat bacteria in the water.

1. What starts the food chain in the deep sea?
2. Why are plants able to grow in shallow waters?
3. What are some plants that grow on land?
4. What are some dark places on land?
5. What creatures live in these dark places?
6. Why are some people afraid of the dark? Are you?

What kinds of animals live in the deep sea?

Many kinds of animals live in the deep sea. Sea stars, sea cucumbers, sea spiders, lobsters, crabs, and sea urchins crawl around looking for food. Glass sponges and sea lilies are attached to the seafloor. Many bottom-dwelling animals, such as worms and heart urchins, bury themselves in the mud. Swimming animals in the deep sea include shrimp, fish, and squid. Many deep-sea creatures eat bits of dead plants and animals that float down from shallower waters.

spider crab

deep-sea angler

1. How do different deep-sea creatures move around?
2. Why has no one ever seen a giant squid alive?
3. Most deep-sea fish have special glowing organs. What do you think these organs are used for?
4. Can you name a land animal that glows?
5. Why do only little bits of food float down to the deep sea?
6. Most deep-sea animals are small and grow very slowly. Why is this?

What are giant tube worms?

Tube worms are long, slender animals that make tubes to live in. Giant tube worms grow in great swarms around hydrothermal vents on the ocean floor. The worms have no mouths or digestive systems and can't "eat." Instead, they get food from bacteria that live inside their bodies. The red tops of tube worms have many blood vessels that *absorb,* or take in, oxygen and sulfur from the vent water. The bacteria use the oxygen and sulfur to make food. Tube worms can grow up to 10 feet long.

1. What body system does a human being have that a tube worm doesn't?
2. Why are the tops of tube worms red?
3. Do you think tube worms are dangerous to other animals on the seafloor?
4. Many kinds of worms build tubes to live in. Why do you think this is?
5. How tall are you? How much taller than you is a 10-foot tube worm?
6. Look around your home. What are some things that come in a tube? What things are wrapped around a tube?

What is the biggest animal in the ocean?

The female blue whale is the biggest animal in the ocean. It is also the largest animal that has ever lived. An adult blue whale can grow up to 100 feet long, about the length of five elephants. It can weigh 150 tons or more, or as much as about 35 elephants. Like all whales, the blue whale is a mammal, not a fish. Its young are called *calves*. At birth, a blue whale calf is already about 23 feet long and weighs about 2 tons.

1. Why do you think it is called a *blue* whale?
2. Can you name some other kinds of whales?
3. What other baby animals are called *calves*?
4. About how many feet will a blue whale calf grow to become an adult whale?
5. Why are some kinds of whales in danger of becoming *extinct,* or disappearing from the Earth?
6. What are some ways people can protect whales from extinction?

What is the biggest fish in the ocean?

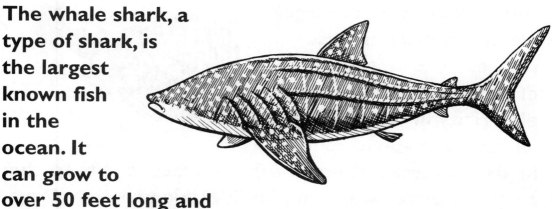

The whale shark, a type of shark, is the largest known fish in the ocean. It can grow to over 50 feet long and weigh about 40 tons. Its coloring is dark bluish gray on its upper body and white on its lower body. It also has white spots and stripes. Whale sharks feed on small fish and animal plankton. They are found in warm, tropical seas around the world. Despite their huge size, whale sharks are harmless to humans and are sometimes called "the gentle giants."

1. Why do you think it is called a *whale* shark?
2. Are there any whale sharks in the Antarctic Ocean?
3. What other kinds of sharks can you name?
4. Why are whale sharks not dangerous to humans?
5. Which ocean animals do you think are most dangerous to humans?
6. Do you know any stories about giants? What are they? Make up your own story about a gentle giant and tell it to a friend or a family member.

Can fish make electricity?

Many fish make electricity, but just three kinds produce large electric shocks: electric rays, electric eels, and electric catfish. Fish make electricity in electric organs, which are made of special kinds of muscles. Electric fish use electric jolts to stun prey and drive away enemies. Electric rays have large, flat bodies and live in the ocean. Electric eels live in South American rivers, and electric catfish live in African rivers. Electric jolts from any of these fish can stun human beings.

electric ray

electric eel

1. What part of an electric fish makes electricity?
2. What would you do if you saw an electric fish swimming near you?
3. Do you think electric fish are fast swimmers or slow swimmers? Why?
4. An electric eel doesn't have to touch its prey to stun it. Why do you think this is?
5. What are some things in your home that use electricity?
6. How do you think people lived their lives before electricity was discovered?

Can sea creatures change color?

Many sea creatures can change color. Flatfish, such as flounder and sole, change their color and pattern to match the seafloor. This helps them lie in wait for prey and avoid predators. Squid and octopuses alter their color to avoid enemies. Cuttlefish, a relative of squid, change color to match their "moods." Cuttlefish change color

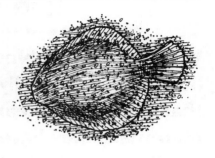

flounder

when they see each other, feel threatened, or spot food. Color-changing animals have bits of color, called *pigments,* in special skin cells. The animals make these skin cells larger or smaller to alter their color.

cuttlefish

1. Why do sea creatures change color?
2. What do you think a flatfish looks like on a sandy seafloor?
3. What is camouflage?
4. Some fish have very bright colors. Why do you think this is?
5. What would you wear if you wanted to hide in a forest? in the snow?
6. A "mood ring" is supposed to change color to match your mood. What color would your ring be when you're happy? sad? excited? angry? hungry? tired?

What kinds of mammals live in the ocean?

Whales and dolphins look like fish, but they are actually mammals that live in the ocean. Like all mammals, they have lungs and breathe air. Seals and walruses are mammals that spend a lot of time in the ocean hunting for food but go to land to have their young. They have webbed flippers for swimming and for waddling about on shore. Seals live in many parts of the world, while walruses are found in the Arctic region. Sea otters are furry, beaverlike mammals with paws on their front legs and flipper-shaped hind feet. They eat and sleep while floating on their backs, and rarely leave the water. Sea otters live in the northern Pacific Ocean.

seal

walrus

1. How do mammals breathe?

2. What are some reptiles that live in the ocean? How do they breathe?

3. What do you think walruses use their tusks for?

4. How do you think sea otters stay warm in the cold waters of the northern Pacific?

5. What are some *characteristics,* or features, of mammals?

6. Most ocean mammals can hold their breath for a long time. How does this help them?

One Step Further

One way whales and dolphins *communicate,* or talk, is by making sounds. To find out how well sound travels through water, try this simple experiment: Get a zipper-lock sandwich bag and fill it with water. Fasten the bag shut, squeezing out as much air as possible. Hold the bag about 6 inches away from your ear and tap the far side of the bag with a large metal spoon. Note how loud the sound is. Now hold the bag up against your ear, and tap it with the large metal spoon again. How is the sound different? Why is it different?

How do sea creatures protect themselves from predators?

Sea creatures use many defenses to protect themselves. Some, such as flatfish, change color to match their surroundings. Others, such as lionfish, have venomous spines that inflict painful stings. Squid and octopuses squirt a cloud of ink to distract enemies while they escape. Clams and snails pull their soft parts into their shells to avoid being eaten. Jellyfish have stinging tentacles, sea urchins are covered with protective spines, and lobsters have hard outer skeletons. Animals without good defenses may hide or swim away quickly.

lionfish

lobster

1. Why do sea creatures need to protect themselves from predators?
2. How do some land animals protect themselves from predators?
3. What does **venomous** mean?
4. What features help ocean predators catch and eat prey?
5. Why do you think decorator crabs cover themselves with pieces of sponge and seaweed?
6. If you felt you were in danger, what would you do to protect yourself?

What are cleaner fish?

Cleaner fish, such as gobies and wrasses, help other fish stay healthy. Cleaners cleanse other fish's wounds and remove pests, called *parasites,* from their bodies. The cleaners' reward is a free meal of parasites. Cleaner fish have areas called *cleaning stations* on coral reefs where their fish "customers" gather to be cleaned. The fish cooperate by remaining still, opening their mouths and gill covers, and not eating the cleaners. Cleaner fish usually have bright stripes and special movements, so that other fish can easily recognize them.

1. How do cleaner fish help other fish?
2. Why do you think fish "customers" don't eat cleaner fish?
3. What do you think false cleaner fish are?
4. Why is it important for people to stay clean?
5. Remoras are fish that use a sucker to attach themselves to larger animals, such as sharks and whales. Why do you think they do this?
6. What are some jobs people have that help other people?

Why do some sea creatures travel long distances?

Some sea creatures travel, or *migrate*, long distances to feed and produce young. Gray whales, for example, spend the summer in the Arctic Ocean eating plankton. When winter comes, the whales migrate about 5,000 miles to the Gulf of California to breed. Eels from rivers in Europe and North America migrate to the Sargasso Sea, in the Atlantic Ocean, to lay eggs. When young eels hatch, they travel to the rivers where their parents lived. Many turtles and seals feed at sea but travel to distant shores to breed.

1. What country is the Gulf of California in?
2. About how many miles do gray whales travel in one year?
3. What are some other animals that migrate?
4. What is an immigrant?
5. How do you think animals know where to go when they're migrating?
6. If you had to migrate to another country, where would you go? Why?

What kinds of products come from the ocean?

Many different products, or *resources,* come from the ocean. People eat seafood, including fish and lobsters. Seaweed is also eaten,

or used to make fertilizer and paint. Sea creatures such as *algae* (AL-jee) and snails are used to make medicines. We get salt from the sea, and valuable metals such as zinc, copper, and iron. Oil is mined from beneath the seafloor and used to make fuel and plastic, and coral and pearls are made into jewelry. We also produce electricity from the movement of tides and waves.

1. What are some other kinds of seafood people eat?
2. A lobster is a type of shellfish. Can you name some other shellfish?
3. What are some other types of metals?
4. Which animals make pearls?
5. What are natural resources?
6. What are some natural resources found on land?

Are the oceans being damaged by people?

Yes, they are being damaged. For many years, people thought they could dump anything into the ocean without causing harm. Scientists found, however, that pollution from oil spills, fertilizers, pesticides, sewage, and industrial wastes harm or kill sea life. Household trash from coastal cities also pollutes the oceans. *Biodegradable* items, such as food products, do less harm because they are broken down by bacteria in the water. But items made of plastic, rubber, and metal aren't broken down. They remain in the ocean or wash up on beaches. Overfishing is another serious problem.

In many parts of the world, too many fish are caught, and fish populations are dying out. Humans must work hard to preserve the oceans, which are important to all life.

1. How does pollution hurt the ocean?
2. What does **biodegradable** mean?
3. What is air pollution?
4. Can you think of some ways to control overfishing?
5. Why are plastic items especially dangerous to sea life?
6. Why are the oceans important to all living things?

One Step Further

Try this experiment to find out what kind of trash is biodegradable.

1. Get the following six items: a piece of orange peel, a steel nail, a cookie, a piece of Styrofoam, a piece of uncoated paper, and a piece of plastic bag.
2. Place each item in a plastic cup and fill all the cups with soil. Label each cup with the name of the item you buried. Water the soil thoroughly and keep it moist until the experiment is completed.
3. Examine each item after one week, two weeks, three weeks, and four weeks. Note any changes in the items you buried. Can you tell which items are biodegradable and which are not?

How do people breathe underwater?

To breathe underwater, scuba divers wear a tank containing compressed air on their backs.

The divers breathe through a mouthpiece attached to a hose that is connected to the tank. Scuba equipment allows divers to descend to about 300 feet. To dive deeper and longer, deep-sea divers wear waterproof suits and helmets, and breathe through a hose connected to an air pump on the surface. For very deep dives, divers wear JIM suits. A JIM suit is part diving suit and part small submersible. It allows divers to breathe normally inside the suit.

1. Why do people need special equipment to breathe underwater?
2. Why are fish able to breathe underwater?
3. How do you think the JIM suit got its name?
4. What is a mermaid?
5. What do you think breath-hold diving is?
6. Would you like to go scuba diving? Why or why not?

Will people ever live under the sea?

It could happen. People are already able to live in underwater habitats for more than a month. To stay beneath the ocean for long periods, however, people will need to get oxygen from seawater. This may soon be possible. Scientists have developed a material that keeps water out but allows oxygen in. This material may allow people to "breathe" underwater. Underwater living could help people study the ocean, farm sea animals and seaweed, and mine valuable ocean minerals.

1. How could people breathe underwater without air tanks?
2. What is a habitat?
3. What do you think a fish farm is?
4. Do you think it would be harder to live on the bottom of the sea or in outer space? Why?
5. Would you like to live under the sea? Why or why not?
6. If people developed "underwater cities," how do you think this might affect the creatures that live in the ocean?

Answers

PAGE 5

1. Blue.
2. Yes.
3. Because most of the Earth is covered with water (oceans), not with land (earth).
4. Because they have a lot of green plants (algae).
5. Because people need oxygen to breathe.
6. The rest is in glaciers, icebergs, lakes, ponds, rivers, and streams. Some water is also found in underground layers of rock called *aquifers*.

PAGE 6

1. The Pacific Ocean.
2. The Antarctic and Arctic oceans have the coldest water because they are in the coldest parts of the world (the South and North Poles, respectively).
3. The Atlantic Ocean. The Indian Ocean.
4. Because all of the Earth's oceans are connected.
5. Sample answers: Continents, mountains, valleys, rivers, lakes, forests, and deserts.
6. Answers will vary.

PAGE 7

1. A billion is bigger (a billion is a thousand million).
2. It means burning hot.
3. The Atlantic Ocean.
4. Hawaii.
5. The ground cannot absorb, or take in, all the rainwater and a flood starts to develop.
6. Answers will vary. Scientists believe the first living things on Earth were simple creatures made of one cell.

PAGES 8–9

1. Something that happens over and over again.
2. Masses of water droplets.
3. They drill wells.
4. Fog.
5. During evaporation, liquid water becomes water vapor gas. During condensation, water vapor gas becomes liquid water.
6. Rainwater washes harmful gases out of the atmosphere (for example, as acid rain).
One Step Further: Water vapor from the bowl will condense on the mirror. The mirror will become covered with drops of water. This is how clouds form.

PAGE 10

1. Flat plains, mountains, volcanoes, and trenches.
2. Both are flat.
3. Sample answers: Rocky Mountains, Appalachian Mountains, Blue Ridge Mountains, Swiss Alps, and Mount Everest.
4. Sample answers: Hawaiian Islands, Caribbean Islands, Samoa, Fiji, Cuba, and Galapagos Islands.
5. There are earthquakes, and mountains form.
6. No, the surface of the moon isn't smooth. It has mountains, plains, craters, and cracks.

PAGE 11

1. The continental shelf.
2. It means to go down suddenly.
3. Both are very steep.
4. Sample answers: To hold books, dishes, and groceries.
5. Answers will vary.
6. Ice shelves are large, flat layers of ice around the margin of a continent. They are found in Antarctica.

PAGE 12

1. The Pacific Ocean.
2. Japan and the Philippines.
3. They are dark and cold because sunlight can't reach those depths.
4. No, plants can't live on the abyssal plains because they're too dark.
5. Sample answers: Grand Canyon, Bryce Canyon, and Zion Canyon.
6. They go down in small submarines or send remote-controlled submarines that carry cameras.

PAGE 13

1. A scientist who studies the oceans.
2. The ocean floor, marine life, the temperature of the water, waves, and currents.
3. Scientists today have many modern instruments to help them.
4. A navy submarine is bigger, stays under-water longer, and is usually used for military purposes, not scientific research.
5–6. Answers will vary.

PAGES 14–15

1. Rainwater picks up salt from rocks and soil, and carries it to the oceans.
2. Sample answers: To flavor food, to preserve food, for baking, and to melt snow and ice on roads in winter.

3. Sample answers: Potato chips, pretzels, nuts, and bacon.
4. Because the water in rivers and lakes isn't salty.
5. Sample answers: Indonesia, India, Kenya, Brazil, and Saudi Arabia.
6. Because seawater is too salty to drink. Too much salt upsets a person's body functions and causes serious harm.
One Step Further: The water will have evaporated and salt will be left behind in the pan. This is similar to what happens in salt pans.

PAGE 16

1. Oceans are larger than seas.
2. More seas.
3. The Atlantic Ocean.
4. Africa and Asia.
5. Sample answers: Seagull, sea horse, sea star, sea urchin, sea anemone, sea cucumber, and sea otter.
6. Lakes are not connected to oceans, and most lakes have fresh water, not salt water.

PAGE 17

1. Because few plants or animals can live in such salty water.
2. Sample answers: Russia, Georgia, Turkey, Bulgaria, Romania, and Ukraine.
3. A little.
4. Motion sickness that occurs when traveling on water.
5. Salty water is very dense, which makes objects more *buoyant*, or more able to float.
6. The White Sea is named for the ice that covers it most of the year.

PAGES 18–19

1. No. Sea level rises and falls.
2. In the Arctic and Antarctic.
3. When the sea level rose, the water covered dead animals that were lying along the coasts.
4. Scientists believe several factors cause ice ages, including the movement of the solar system in space, changes in the Earth's rotation, and continental drift.
5. Ice sheets will melt, raising the sea level and causing flooding along coastal areas.
6. Answers will vary.
One Step Further: The water in the "greenhouse jar" will be warmer because the plastic bag traps the heat of the sun or lamp and holds it in.

PAGE 20

1. An estuary contains salt water mixed with fresh water, while the open sea contains only salt water.
2. Sample answers: Oak, elm, maple, birch, and palm.
3. Sample answers: Mississippi, Missouri, Colorado, Rio Grande, Amazon, Congo, Nile, and St. Lawrence.
4. Lighthouses guide ships traveling in coastal waters, and warn them of dangers such as shallow water and rocks.
5–6. Answers will vary.

PAGE 21

1. Two.
2. A swollen or expanded area.
3. A high tide is coming in.
4. High tide brings deep water to ports, so large ships can travel in and out more easily.
5. During low tide, because more of the beach area is exposed.
6. Because the Sun is much farther from the Earth than the Moon is, and gravitational attraction is weaker when objects are farther apart.

PAGE 22

1. No. During high tide, all of the rocky shore is underwater.
2. On the bottom, the rocks, and the plants, and in the water.
3. Seaweeds provide food and shelter for tide pool animals.
4. Rocky shores trap water between rocks. Sandy shores can't trap water.
5. No. The kind of life in a tide pool depends on its location and size, and the climate of the area.
6. Sample answers: They're brought in with the tide; small algae are carried in on the feet of birds; seabirds accidentally drop fish or other animals in; the wind blows them in.

PAGE 23

1. How fast, how long, and how far the wind blows.
2. Answers will vary. (The tallest recorded wind-blown wave was 112 feet—as high as a 10-story building.)
3. Huge waves can dump tons of water onto a ship, breaking it apart.
4. No, it can't. Water doesn't move forward with a wave.
5. No. Their energy decreases with depth.
6. Waves can wear away rocks on a coastline. They can also move sand around to create beaches and sand dunes.

PAGES 24–25

1. Surface currents are near the top of the ocean, and deep-water currents are near the bottom of the ocean.
2. Yes.
3. Some fast currents can carry swimmers away.
4. Answers will vary.
5. Because the fresh water of the river is less dense than the salt water of the ocean.
6. Scientists studied the shoes' movement, and where they were eventually found, to learn about ocean currents.

One Step Further: The hot water will float on the cold water. In the ocean, warm-water currents flow above denser cold-water currents.

PAGE 26

1. Answers will vary.
2. Oregon, Nevada, and Arizona.
3. Sample answers: Hot, cold, sunny, cloudy, rainy, windy, chilly, and humid.
4. Sample answers: Thunderstorms, snowstorms, blizzards, windstorms, typhoons, and cyclones.
5. Warm currents come from hot places, such as the equator. Cold currents come from cold places, such as the North and South Poles.
6. Sample answers: Biology, geology, psychology, zoology, and anthropology.

PAGE 27

1. A change in wind patterns.
2. Answers will vary.
3. Sample answers: Eastern Pacific Ocean—United States, Canada, Mexico, and Peru. Western Pacific Ocean—Japan, China, and Australia.
4. During an El Niño, there's not enough food for fish, so they die. This leaves fewer fish in the ocean for the fishing industry to catch, and hurts their business.
5. Sample answers: There isn't enough water, so crops die and people starve; rivers and lakes dry up, killing the plants and animals that live there.
6. Because the damaging effects of an El Niño are felt in many places.

PAGE 28

1. Over oceans, near the equator.
2. Strong hurricane winds travel much faster.
3. Storm warnings, issued by the National Weather Service, tell people that a dangerous storm may be headed their way.
4. Storm warnings are broadcast so people can prepare themselves and their homes, or leave areas in the storm's path.

5. Sample answers: Board up the windows, get a portable radio, get flashlights and candles, have extra food and water handy.
6. Answers will vary.

PAGE 29

1. No. The waters in the Arctic Ocean are very cold, and waterspouts usually develop over warm seas.
2. It means spinning around very fast.
3. A swirling circle of water with a depression in the middle that draws floating objects toward it.
4. Both are whirling columns of air. A waterspout occurs over water, and a tornado forms over land.
5. It carried Dorothy and Toto from Kansas to Oz.
6. They can carry fish and other things sucked up from the ocean.

PAGE 30

1. An undersea earthquake, landslide, or volcanic eruption.
2. Because a tidal wave, or tsunami, is not produced by the tides.
3. 300 miles.
4. It is in the Pacific Ocean, just north of Australia.
5. Yes. Scientists know when major underwater activity has occurred, such as earthquakes and volcanic eruptions, and they know this activity causes tsunamis.
6. By measuring the height of debris from the tsunami on buildings and trees, or measuring the height of water stains.

PAGE 31

1. Because rip currents have nothing to do with the tides.
2. Away from shore.
3. It means to come together and move through a narrow opening.
4. Sample answers: Look for a flow of murky water; choppy waves; foam or objects moving out to sea; a break in the line of incoming waves.
5. Don't panic or swim against the current. Swim parallel to the shore to break free of it, or relax and let it carry you out past the opening in the underwater obstacle, to where the water becomes calmer.
6. Sample answers: Swim, surf, build sandcastles, look for seashells, and lie in the sun.

PAGE 32

1. About nine-tenths.
2. Because most of an iceberg is underwater and can't be seen. A ship might accidentally run into the submerged ice.

3. The *Titanic*.
4. An icebreaker is a ship that can smash through ice. It is used to clear a path through ice-covered waters, and to explore the Arctic and Antarctic regions.
5. Sample answers: Arctic animals include seals, whales, polar bears, arctic foxes, arctic wolves, and walruses. Antarctic animals include whales, penguins, and seals.
6. Sea level would rise all over the world, and coastal areas now above sea level would be underwater.

PAGE 33
1. Hard.
2. No, because the water is too cold.
3. It is coral that looks similar to a human brain. Brain coral has ridges and grooves, and a rounded shape.
4. It provides a place for them to hide from predators.
5. *Coral* is a hard limestone cup built by polyps. A *corral* is a fenced holding area for horses or other livestock.
6. Algae make food for the polyps. The polyps provide a home for the algae.

PAGE 34
1. Papua New Guinea.
2. A protected area of water where fishing and other activities are limited or not allowed.
3. About 6 years.
4. Sample answers: The Grand Canyon, the Statue of Liberty, Yellowstone National Park, the White House, and Disney World.
5. Sample answers: Visitors might step on reefs or break off pieces of coral as souvenirs; pollution could make the reef animals sick or kill them.
6. Because the reef roughly follows the Australian coastline and acts as a barrier, or block, between the water along the shore and the open sea.

PAGE 35
1. Phytoplankton are plants and zooplankton are animals.
2. It makes things look bigger.
3. Sample answers: Seaweeds and sea grasses.
4. Land plants need roots to take up water from the ground. Sea plants can absorb water directly from the ocean.
5. Answers will vary.
6. There wouldn't be enough food for larger animals, and eventually most ocean animals would die.

PAGES 36–37
1. Yes. Humans eat plants and animals.
2. Because phytoplankton need sunlight to live, and the deep sea gets no sunlight.
3. A meat-eater, or an animal that eats other animals.
4. It is the animal at the top of the food chain, which isn't eaten by other animals (until it dies).
5. They help to "recycle" the remains of dead animals by returning the useful particles in the dead creatures to the environment.
6. It would hurt the food chain because small fish are food for other animals, which might die of starvation without them.

PAGE 38
1. A sandy shore.
2. An animal that hunts and kills other animals for food.
3. Yes, because many animals on sandy shores hide in the sand.
4. Sea otters can use their sharp teeth and strong front paws to crack open the shells, or they might hold a rock against their chest and smash the shellfish against it.
5. When a crab gets too big for its shell, it sheds the shell and grows a larger one.
6. At low tide, there is no water to cover the animals and they must dig deeper into the sand. At high tide, fish may eat the shore animals.

PAGE 39
1. In ponds, lakes, streams, rivers, and oceans.
2. Sample answers: Birds, frogs, insects, and most snakes.
3. Sample answers: Tuna, salmon, flounder, trout, haddock, cod, and halibut.
4. Sample answers: Mammals, birds, reptiles, and amphibians.
5. Because starfish are not fish.
6. To communicate with other fish or to scare away enemies.

PAGE 40
1. A caudal fin.
2. Its pectoral fins and pelvic fins.
3. Flying fish can propel themselves out of the water with their strong tails. They glide through the air above the water, spreading out their fins like wings.
4. We mean that the person is very comfortable in the water and swims well.
5. To reduce water resistance.
6. Sample answers: Airplanes, trains, race cars, and speedboats.

PAGE 41
1. By breathing air.
2. The heart.
3. Both lungs and gills take in oxygen and send out carbon dioxide.
4. Lungs absorb oxygen from air. Gills absorb oxygen from water.
5. Lungfish are air-breathing fish that must rise to the surface to breathe.
6. Tadpoles live only in water. Adult frogs live both in water and on land.

PAGE 42
1. Sulfur-containing minerals.
2. It means burning hot or almost boiling.
3. Yes. They are called *geysers*.
4. So the smoke and heat from the fire can escape to the outside.
5. Because the murky water shooting up looks like smoke.
6. White smokers are chimneys made of light-colored minerals.

PAGE 43
1. Bacteria.
2. Because sunlight can penetrate the water and reach the plants.
3. Sample answers: Trees, shrubs, grasses, and flowers.
4. Sample answers: Caves, tunnels, and burrows.
5. Sample answers: Spiders, insects, bats, and moles.
6. Answers will vary.

PAGE 44
1. Some crawl and some swim.
2. Because giant squid live in the ocean depths. We know they exist only because a few dead ones have washed up on beaches.
3. To attract mates and smaller animals to eat.
4. A firefly.
5. Because most are eaten on the way down.
6. Because food is very scarce in the deep sea.

PAGE 45
1. A digestive system.
2. Because they have many blood vessels, which are red.
3. They probably aren't dangerous, because they can't eat other animals.
4. To support their soft bodies and to protect them.
5. Answers will vary.
6. Sample answers: In a tube—toothpaste, face creams, and ointments. Around a tube—toilet paper, paper towels, and wrapping paper.

PAGE 46
1. Because its skin is blue-gray in color, with some white speckles.
2. Sample answers: Humpback, sperm, gray, beluga, and killer whales.
3. Sample answers: Cows, elephants, giraffes, and rhinoceroses.

4. About 77 feet.
5. Because the whaling industry catches and kills so many, and because of water pollution.
6. Answers will vary.

PAGE 47

1. Because it is so large. Whale sharks can grow bigger than several species of whales.
2. No, because the water in the Antarctic Ocean is too cold.
3. Sample answers: Great white, tiger, sand, hammerhead, mako, bull, and lemon.
4. Because whale sharks eat only very small sea creatures.
5. Sample answers: Several species of sharks, stingrays, sea snakes, barracudas, and sea wasps (jellyfish with deadly stingers).
6. Answers will vary.

PAGE 48

1. Electric organs.
2. You should swim away from it.
3. Most are slow swimmers. They don't need to chase prey or flee from predators because they can stop them with an electric shock.
4. Because electricity can travel through water.
5. Sample answers: Lamp, television, stereo, computer, electric stove, refrigerator, toaster, and hair dryer.
6. Answers will vary.

PAGE 49

1. To avoid predators, lie in wait for prey, or match their "moods."
2. It has speckled, light-brown coloring.
3. A pattern or coloring that blends in with the surroundings.
4. Sample answers: To attract mates, to warn predators (if the fish is poisonous), to lure prey, or to warn other animals away from their territory.
5. You would wear clothes in shades of green or brown to hide in a forest, and white clothes to hide in the snow.
6. Answers will vary.

PAGES 50–51

1. With their lungs.
2. Sample answers: Sea turtles, saltwater crocodiles, and sea snakes. Reptiles breathe with lungs.
3. Sample answers: To defend themselves from predators, to haul themselves onto the Arctic ice from the water, and to dig out shellfish from the ocean floor.
4. Their thick layer of fur acts as insulation by trapping air and keeping their skin dry.

5. Sample answers: Mammals have hair (sometimes just bristles on their snouts), produce milk to feed their young, are warm-blooded, and have larger brains than other kinds of animals.
6. It allows them to stay underwater longer, and dive deeper, as they search for food.
One Step Further: The sound will be louder when the bag is held next to the ear. This is because sound travels through water better than it travels through air.

PAGE 52

1. To avoid being eaten.
2. Sample answers: Porcupines have long, sharp quills; armadillos have bony plates; tortoises have hard shells; skunks have a bad-smelling spray; and deer run fast.
3. It means containing poison.
4. Sample answers: Predators may have strong teeth or claws to crack open animal shells; they may deliver electric shocks or venomous bites; they may swim fast; or they may hunt in groups.
5. To disguise themselves, so predators won't see them.
6. Answers will vary.

PAGE 53

1. They clean their wounds and remove parasites from their bodies.
2. Because they know the cleaner fish are helping them.
3. False cleaner fish look like real cleaner fish. They attract fish customers, then take a bite of their fins or scales.
4. To reduce the chance of getting infections and illnesses.
5. Remoras get a free ride from the larger animals and eat the scraps of food left by their "hosts." In return, the remoras eat parasites on the animals' skin.
6. Sample answers: Nurse, doctor, firefighter, police officer, and teacher.

PAGE 54

1. Mexico.
2. About 10,000 miles.
3. Sample answers: Birds, salmon, monarch butterflies, and caribou.
4. A person who leaves one country and goes to another country to live.
5. Scientists believe many animals have instincts, or inborn knowledge, that tell them where to go. To find their way, they might use smell, the Earth's magnetic field, the stars, the Moon, or the Sun.
6. Answers will vary.

PAGE 55

1. Sample answers: Shrimp, clams, crabs, turtles, sharks, whales, and octopuses.

2. Sample answers: Clams, crabs, oysters, and shrimp.
3. Sample answers: Gold, silver, nickel, lead, aluminum, and tin.
4. Oysters.
5. Usable materials or energy supplied by nature.
6. Sample answers: Lumber; gold, silver, and other minerals; oil and natural gas; and soil.

PAGES 56–57

1. It harms or kills ocean animals.
2. It means an object is capable of being broken down by small organisms, such as bacteria.
3. Air pollution is contamination of the atmosphere by soot and gases from power plants, cars, trucks, industrial plants, and other sources.
4. Sample answer: Countries could sign an agreement to stop overfishing by putting a limit on how much fish can be caught.
5. Sea animals mistake plastic items for food and eat them. The plastic can get caught in an animal's throat or create a block in its stomach and kill the animal.
6. Sample answers: Many food chains start with plankton; algae produce oxygen; animals need salt to live; and the ocean is part of the water cycle, which provides fresh water (rain) for plants and animals.
One Step Further: The piece of orange peel and the cookie will degrade the fastest. The piece of plastic and the Styrofoam are not biodegradable and will not change.

PAGE 58

1. Because people breathe with lungs, which are designed to get oxygen from air, not water.
2. Because fish have gills, which are designed to absorb oxygen from water.
3. It is named after Jim Jarratt, an early underwater explorer.
4. A mythical creature, half human female and half fish, that lives in the sea.
5. Diving without special breathing equipment. Breath-hold divers take a deep breath at the surface, then dive underwater.
6. Answers will vary.

PAGE 59

1. By using a material that lets oxygen in but keeps water out.
2. The place or environment where a person, animal, or plant lives.
3. A place where large numbers of fish are raised, so they can be sold.
4–6. Answers will vary.

Other **Gifted & Talented®**

books that will help develop your child's gifts and talents

Workbooks:

- Reading (4–6) $4.95
- Reading Book Two (4–6) $4.95
- Math (4–6) $4.95
- Math Book Two (4–6) $4.95
- Language Arts (4–6) $4.95
- Language Arts Puzzles & Games (4–6) $4.95
- Puzzles & Games for Reading and Math (4–6) $4.95
- Puzzles & Games for Reading and Math Book Two (4–6) $4.95
- Puzzles & Games for Critical and Creative Thinking (4–6) $4.95
- Phonics (4–6) $4.95
- Phonics Puzzles & Games (4–6) $4.95
- Math Puzzles & Games (4–6) $4.95
- Reading Puzzles & Games (4–6) $4.95
- Reading (6–8) $4.95
- Reading Book Two (6–8) $4.95
- Math (6–8) $4.95
- Math Book Two (6–8) $4.95
- Language Arts (6–8) $4.95
- Puzzles & Games for Reading and Math (6–8) $4.95
- Puzzles & Games for Reading and Math Book Two (6–8) $4.95
- Puzzles & Games for Critical and Creative Thinking (6–8) $4.95
- Phonics (6–8) $4.95
- Phonics Puzzles & Games (6–8) $4.95
- Math Puzzles & Games (6–8) $4.95
- Reading Puzzles & Games (6–8) $4.95
- Reading Comprehension (6–8) $4.95
- Reading Comprehension Book Two (6–8) $4.95

For Preschoolers:

- Alphabet Workbook $5.95
- Counting Workbook $5.95
- Word Workbook $5.95
- Animals Workbook $5.95
- Colors Workbook $5.95

Reference Workbooks:

- Word Book (4–6) $4.95
- Almanac (6–8) $3.95
- Animal Almanac (6–8) $6.95
- Atlas (6–8) $3.95
- Dictionary (6–8) $3.95

Science Workbooks:

- The Human Body (4–6) $5.95
- Animals (4–6) $5.95
- The Earth (4–6) $5.95
- The Ocean (4–6) $5.95
- Dinosaurs (6–8) $5.95
- Reptiles & Amphibians (6–8) $5.95
- Science Experiments (6–8) $5.95

Question & Answer Books:

- The Gifted & Talented® Question & Answer Book for Ages 4–6 $5.95
- Gifted & Talented® More Questions & Answers for Ages 4–6 $5.95
- Gifted & Talented® Still More Questions & Answers for Ages 4–6 $5.95
- The Gifted & Talented® Question & Answer Book for Ages 6–8 $5.95
- Gifted & Talented® More Questions & Answers for Ages 6–8 $5.95
- Gifted & Talented® Still More Questions & Answers for Ages 6–8 $5.95
- Gifted & Talented® Science Questions & Answers: The Human Body for Ages 6–8 $5.95
- Gifted & Talented® Science Questions & Answers: Animals for Ages 6–8 $5.95
- Gifted & Talented® Science Questions & Answers: The Ocean for Ages 6–8 $5.95

Story Starters:

- My First Stories (6–8) $5.95
- Stories About Me (6–8) $5.95
- Stories About Animals (6–8) $4.95
- Mysteries (6–8) $5.95

For orders, call 1-800-323-4900.